GOOGLE CLOUD PROFESSIONAL CLOUD SECURITY ENGINEER EXAM PRACTICE QUESTIONS & DUMPS

EXAM STUDY GUIDE FOR PROFESSIONAL CLOUD SECURITY ENGINEER EXAM PREP LATEST VERSION

Presented By: Quantic Books

About Quantic Books:

Quantic Books is a publishing house based in Princeton, New Jersey, USA. , a platform that is accessible online as well as locally, which gives power to educational content, erudite collection, poetry & many other book genres. We make it easy for writers & authors to get their books designed, published, promoted, and sell professionally on worldwide scale with eBook + Print distribution. Quantic Books is now distributing books worldwide.

Note: Find answers of the questions at the last of the book.

QUESTION 1

When making a protected container image, which two objects must you join into the build if likely? (Select two.)

A. Make sure that the app does not run as PID 1.
B. Package a single app as a container.
C. Eliminate any unwanted tools not required by the app.
D. Use public container images as a base image for the app.
E. Use many container image layers to cover sensitive information.

QUESTION 2

A corporation is running workloads in a devoted server room. They needs to only be opened from within the private corporation network. You need to connect to these workloads from Compute Engine instances within a Google Cloud Platform project.

Which two tactics can you take to meet the necessities? (Select two.)

A. Organize the project with Cloud VPN.
B. Organize the project with Shared VPC.
C. Organize the project with Cloud Interconnect.
D. Organize the project with VPC peering.
E. Organize all Compute Engine instances with Private Access.

QUESTION 3

A client executes Cloud Identity-Aware Proxy for their ERP system hosted on Compute Engine. Their security crew necessitates to add a security layer so that the ERP systems only accept traffic from Cloud Identity-Aware Proxy.

What must the client do to meet these necessities?

A. Make sure that the ERP system can authenticate the JWT assertion in the HTTP requests.
B. Make sure that the ERP system can authenticate the identity headers in the HTTP requests.
C. Make sure that the ERP system can authenticate the x-forwarded-for headers in the HTTP requests.
D. Make sure that the ERP system can authenticate the user's unique identifier headers in the HTTP requests.

QUESTION 4

A client needs to avert attackers from hijacking their domain/IP

and redirecting users to a malicious site through a man-in-the-

middle attack. Which result must this client use?

A. VPC Flow Logs
B. Cloud Armor
C. DNS Security Extensions
D. Cloud Identity-Aware Proxy

QUESTION 5

A client deploys an application to App Engine and needs to check for Open Web Application Security Project (OWASP) susceptibilities. Which service must be used to do this?

A. Cloud Armor
B. Google Cloud Audit Logs
C. Cloud Security Scanner
D. Forseti Security

QUESTION 6

A client's data science group necessitates to use Google Cloud Platform (GCP) for their analytics workloads. Corporation policy commands that all data needs to be corporation owned and all user verifications needs to go through their own Security Assertion Markup Language (SAML) 2.0 Identity Provider (IdP). The Infrastructure Operations Systems Engineer was trying to set up Cloud Identity for the client and realized that their domain was already being used by G Suite.

How must you best advise the Systems Engineer to proceed with the least disruption?

A. Contact Google Support and instigate the Domain Contestation Process to use the domain name in your new Cloud Identity domain.
B. Register a new domain name, and use that for the new Cloud Identity domain.
C. Ask Google to provision the data science manager's account as a Super Administrator in the existing domain.
D. Ask client's management to ascertain any other uses of Google managed services, and work with the existing Super Administrator.

QUESTION 7

An application running on a Compute Engine instance needs to read data from a Cloud Storage bucket. Your crew does not allow Cloud Storage buckets to be globally readable and necessitates to make sure the principle of least opportunity.

Which option meets the necessity of your crew?

A. Make a Cloud Storage ACL that lets read-only access from the Compute Engine instance's IP address and lets the application to read from the bucket without credentials.

B. Use a service account with read-only access to the Cloud Storage bucket, and store the credentials to the service account in the config of the application on the Compute Engine instance.

C. Use a service account with read-only access to the Cloud Storage bucket to retrieve the credentials from the instance metadata.

D. Encrypt the data in the Cloud Storage bucket using Cloud KMS, and allow the application to decrypt the data with the KMS key.

QUESTION 8

An boss necessitates to track how bonus compensations have changed over time to find worker outliers and right earning disparities. This task needs to be performed without revealing the sensitive compensation data for any individual and needs to be reversible to find the outlier.

Which Cloud Data Loss Prevention API method must you use to do this?

A. Generalization
B. Redaction
C. CryptoHashConfig
D. CryptoReplaceFfxFpeConfig

QUESTION 9

You need to follow Google-suggested practices to leverage

envelope encryption and encrypt data at the application layer.

What must you do?

A. Make a data encryption key (DEK) locally to encrypt the data, and make a new key encryption key (KEK) in Cloud KMS to encrypt the DEK. Store both the encrypted data and the encrypted DEK.

B. Make a data encryption key (DEK) locally to encrypt the data, and make a new key encryption key (KEK) in Cloud KMS to encrypt the DEK. Store both the encrypted data and the KEK.

C. Make a new data encryption key (DEK) in Cloud KMS to encrypt the data, and make a key encryption key (KEK) locally to encrypt the key. Store both the encrypted data and the encrypted DEK.

D. Make a new data encryption key (DEK) in Cloud KMS to encrypt the data, and make a key encryption key (KEK) locally to encrypt the key. Store both the encrypted data and the KEK.

QUESTION 10

How must a client consistently deliver Stackdriver logs from GCP to their on-premises SIEM system?

A. Send all logs to the SIEM system via an existing protocol such as syslog.

B. Organize every project to export all their logs to a common BigQuery DataSet, which will be queried by the SIEM system.

C. Organize Organizational Log Sinks to export logs to a Cloud Pub/Sub Topic, which will be sent to the SIEM via Dataflow.

D. Build a connector for the SIEM to query for all logs in real time from the GCP RESTful JSON APIs.

QUESTION 11

When working with agents in a support center via online chat, an organization's clients time and again share pictures of their documents with personally identifiable information (PII). The organization that possesses the support center is concerned that the PII is being stored in their databases as part of the regular chat logs they retain for review by internal or external analysts for client service trend analysis.

Which Google Cloud result must the organization use to help resolve this concern for the client while still maintaining data utility?

A. Use Cloud Key Management Service (KMS) to encrypt the PII data shared by clients before storing it for analysis.

B. Use Object Lifecycle Management to make sure that all chat records with PII in them are discarded and not saved for analysis.

C. Use the image inspection and redaction actions of the DLP API to redact PII from the images before storing them for analysis.

D. Use the generalization and bucketing actions of the DLP API result to redact PII from the texts before storing them for analysis.

QUESTION 12

A corporation's application is deployed with a user-managed Service Account key. You want to use Google-suggested practices to rotate the key. What must you do?

A. Open Cloud Shell and run `gcloud iam service-accounts enable-auto-rotate --iam-account=IAM_ACCOUNT`.

B. Open Cloud Shell and run `gcloud iam service-accounts keys rotate --iam-account=IAM_ACCOUNT --key=NEW_KEY`.

C. Make a new key, and use the new key in the application. Delete the old key from the Service Account.

D. Make a new key, and use the new key in the application. Store the old key on the system as a backup key.

QUESTION 13

An organization is migrating from their current on-premises productivity software systems to G Suite. Some network security controls were in place that were mandated by a regulatory body in their region for their previous on-premises system. The organization's risk crew necessitates to make sure that network security controls are maintained and effective in G Suite. A security architect supporting this migration has been asked to make sure that network security controls are in place as part of the new shared responsibility model among the organization and Google Cloud.

What result would help meet the necessities?

A. Make sure that firewall rules are in place to meet the necessary controls.

B. Set up Cloud Armor to make sure that network security controls can be managed for G Suite.

C. Network security is a built-in result and Google's Cloud responsibility for SaaS products like G Suite.

D. Set up an array of Virtual Private Cloud (VPC) networks to control network security as mandated by the relevant regulation.

QUESTION 14

A client's corporation has multiple business units. Each business unit operates independently, and each has their own engineering group. Your crew wants visibility into all projects made within the corporation and necessitates to organize their Google Cloud Platform (GCP) projects based on different business units. Each business unit also necessitates separate sets of IAM permissions.

Which strategy must you use to meet these needs?

A. Make an organization node, and assign folders for each business unit.
B. Establish standalone projects for each business unit, using gmail.com accounts.
C. Assign GCP resources in a project, with a label classifying which business unit possesses the resource.
D. Assign GCP resources in a VPC for each business unit to separate network access.

QUESTION 15

A corporation has redundant mail servers in different Google Cloud Platform regions and necessitates to route clients to the nearest mail server based on location. How must the corporation do this?

A. Organize TCP Proxy Load Balancing as a global load balancing service listening on port 995.
B. Make a Network Load Balancer to listen on TCP port 995 with a forwarding rule to forward traffic based on location.
C. Use Cross-Region Load Balancing with an HTTP(S) load balancer to route traffic to the nearest region.
D. Use Cloud CDN to route the mail traffic to the closest origin mail server based on client IP address.

QUESTION 16

Your crew sets up a Shared VPC Network where project co-vpc-prod is the host project. Your crew has organized the firewall rules, subnets, and VPN gateway on the host project. They need to enable Engineering Group A to attach a Compute Engine instance to only the 10.1.1.0/24 subnet.

What must your crew grant to Engineering Group A to meet this necessity?

A. Compute Network User Role at the host project level.
B. Compute Network User Role at the subnet level.
C. Compute Shared VPC Admin Role at the host project level.
D. Compute Shared VPC Admin Role at the service project level.

QUESTION 17

An organization is starting to move its infrastructure from its on-premises environment to Google Cloud Platform (GCP). The first step the organization necessitates to take is to migrate its current data backup and disaster recovery results to GCP for later analysis. The organization's production environment will remain on-premises for an indefinite time. The organization wants a scalable and cost-efficient result.

Which GCP result must the organization use?

A. BigQuery using a data pipeline job with continuous updates
B. Cloud Storage using a scheduled task and gsutil
C. Compute Engine Virtual Machines using Persistent Disk
D. Cloud Datastore using regularly scheduled batch upload jobs

QUESTION 18

You are making an internal App Engine application that needs to access a user's Google Drive on the user's behalf. Your corporation does not want to rely on the current user's credentials. It also necessitates to follow Google-suggested practices.

What must you do?

A. Make a new Service account, and give all application users the role of Service Account User.
B. Make a new Service account, and add all application users to a Google Group. Give this group the role of Service Account User.
C. Use a steadfast G Suite Admin account, and validate the application's operations with these G Suite credentials.
D. Make a new service account, and grant it G Suite domain-wide delegation. Have the application use it to impersonate the user.

QUESTION 19

A client necessitates to move their sensitive workloads to a Compute Engine-based cluster using Managed Instance Groups (MIGs). The jobs are bursty and needs to be completed quickly. They have a necessity to be able to manage and rotate the encryption keys.

Which boot disk encryption result must you use on the cluster to meet this client's necessities?

A. Client-supplied encryption keys (CSEK)
B. Client-managed encryption keys (CMEK) using Cloud Key Management Service (KMS)
C. Encryption by default
D. Pre-encrypting files before transferring to Google Cloud Platform (GCP) for analysis

QUESTION 20

A client's internal security crew needs to manage its own encryption keys for encrypting data on Cloud Storage and decides to use client-supplied encryption keys (CSEK).

How must the crew complete this task?

A. Upload the encryption key to a Cloud Storage bucket, and then upload the object to the same bucket.
B. Use the gsutil command line tool to upload the object to Cloud Storage, and specify the location of the encryption key.
C. Make an encryption key in the Google Cloud Platform Console, and upload an object to Cloud Storage using the specified key.
D. Encrypt the object, then use the gsutil command line tool or the Google Cloud Platform Console to upload the object to Cloud Storage.

QUESTION 21

A client has 300 engineers. The corporation necessitates to grant different levels of access and efficiently manage IAM permissions among users in the development and production environment projects.

Which two steps must the corporation take to meet these necessities? (Select two.)

A. Make a project with multiple VPC networks for each environment.
B. Make a folder for each development and production environment.
C. Make a Google Group for the Engineering crew, and assign permissions at the folder level.
D. Make an Organizational Policy constraint for each folder environment.
E. Make projects for each environment, and grant IAM rights to each engineering user.

QUESTION 22

A DevOps crew will make a new container to run on Google Kubernetes Engine. As the application will be internet-facing, they want to minimize the attack surface of the container.

What must they do?

A. Use Cloud Build to build the container images.
B. Build small containers using small base images.
C. Delete non-used versions from Container Registry.
D. Use a Continuous Delivery tool to deploy the application.

QUESTION 23

While migrating your organization's infrastructure to GCP, a large number of users will need to access GCP Console. The Identity Management crew already has a well-established way to manage your users and want to keep using your existing Active Directory or LDAP server along with the existing SSO password.

What must you do?

A. Manually synchronize the data in Google domain with your existing Active Directory or LDAP server.
B. Use Google Cloud Directory Sync to synchronize the data in Google domain with your existing Active Directory or LDAP server.
C. Users sign in directly to the GCP Console using the credentials from your on-premises Kerberos compliant identity provider.
D. Users sign in using OpenID (OIDC) compatible IdP, receive an verification token, then use that token to log in to the GCP Console.

QUESTION 24

Your corporation is using GSuite and has developed an application meant for internal usage on Google App Engine. You need to make sure that an external user cannot gain access to the application even when an worker's password has been compromised.

What must you do?

A. Enforce 2-factor verification in GSuite for all users.
B. Organize Cloud Identity-Aware Proxy for the App Engine Application.
C. Provision user passwords using GSuite Password Sync.
D. Organize Cloud VPN among your private network and GCP.

QUESTION 25

A corporation is deploying their application on Google Cloud Platform. Corporation policy necessitates long-term data to be stored using a result that can automatically replicate data over at least two geographic places.

Which Storage result are they allowed to use?

A. Cloud Bigtable
B. Cloud BigQuery
C. Compute Engine SSD Disk
D. Compute Engine Persistent Disk

QUESTION 26

A large e-retailer is moving to Google Cloud Platform with its ecommerce website. The corporation necessitates to make sure payment information is encrypted among the client's browser and GCP when the clients checkout online.

What must they do?

A. Organize an SSL Certificate on an L7 Load Balancer and require encryption.
B. Organize an SSL Certificate on a Network TCP Load Balancer and require encryption.
C. Organize the firewall to allow inbound traffic on port 443, and block all other inbound traffic.
D. Organize the firewall to allow outbound traffic on port 443, and block all other outbound traffic.

QUESTION 27

You are in charge of migrating a legacy application from your corporation datacenters to GCP before the current maintenance contract expires. You do not know what ports the application is using and no documentation is available for you to check. You want to complete the migration without putting your environment at risk.

What must you do?

A. Migrate the application into an isolated project using a "Lift & Shift" approach. Enable all internal TCP traffic using VPC Firewall rules. Use VPC Flow logs to determine what traffic must be allowed for the application to work properly.

B. Migrate the application into an isolated project using a "Lift & Shift" approach in a custom network. Disable all traffic within the VPC and look at the Firewall logs to determine what traffic must be allowed for the application to work properly.

C. Refactor the application into a micro-services architecture in a GKE cluster. Disable all traffic from outside the cluster using Firewall Rules. Use VPC Flow logs to determine what traffic must be allowed for the application to work properly.

D. Refactor the application into a micro-services architecture hosted in Cloud Functions in an isolated project. Disable all traffic from outside your project using Firewall Rules. Use VPC Flow logs to determine what traffic must be allowed for the application to work properly.

QUESTION 28

Your corporation has deployed an application on Compute Engine. The application is accessible by clients on port 587. You need to balance the load among the different instances running the application. The connection must be protected using TLS, and terminated by the Load Balancer.

What type of Load Balancing must you use?

A. Network Load Balancing
B. HTTP(S) Load Balancing
C. TCP Proxy Load Balancing
D. SSL Proxy Load Balancing

QUESTION 29

Your crew needs to avert users from making projects in the

organization. Only the DevOps crew must be allowed to make

projects on behalf of the requester. Which two tasks must your

crew perform to handle this request? (Select two.)

A. Eliminate all users from the Project Creator role at the organizational level.
B. Make an Organization Policy constraint, and apply it at the organizational level.
C. Grant the Project Editor role at the organizational level to a designated group of users.
D. Add a designated group of users to the Project Creator role at the organizational level.
E. Grant the billing account creator role to the designated DevOps crew.

QUESTION 30

A client deployed an application on Compute Engine that takes advantage of the elastic nature of cloud computing.

How can you work with Infrastructure Operations Engineers to best make sure that Windows Compute Engine VMs are up to date with all the latest OS patches?

A. Build new base images when patches are available, and use a CI/CD pipeline to rebuild VMs, deploying incrementally.
B. Federate a Domain Controller into Compute Engine, and roll out weekly patches via Group Policy Object.
C. Use Deployment Manager to provision updated VMs into new serving Instance Groups (IGs).
D. Reboot all VMs for the duration of the weekly maintenance window and allow the StartUp Script to download the latest patches from the internet.

QUESTION 31

An organization receives an increasing number of phishing emails.

Which method must be used to protect worker credentials in this situation?

A. Multifactor Verification
B. A strict password policy
C. Captcha on login pages
D. Encrypted emails

QUESTION 32

A client is collaborating with another corporation to build an application on Compute Engine. The client is building the application tier in their GCP Organization, and the other corporation is building the storage tier in a different GCP Organization. This is a 3-tier web application. Communication among portions of the application needs to not traverse the public internet by any means.

Which connectivity option must be implemented?

A. VPC peering
B. Cloud VPN
C. Cloud Interconnect
D. Shared VPC

QUESTION 33

Your crew necessitates to make sure Compute Engine instances running in your production project do not have public IP addresses. The frontend application Compute Engine instances will require public IPs. The product engineers have the Editor role to modify resources. Your crew necessitates to enforce this necessity.

How must your crew meet these necessities?

A. Enable Private Access on the VPC network in the production project.
B. Eliminate the Editor role and grant the Compute Admin IAM role to the engineers.
C. Set up an organization policy to only permit public IPs for the front-end Compute Engine instances.
D. Set up a VPC network with two subnets: one with public IPs and one without public IPs.

QUESTION 34

A patch for a vulnerability has been released, and a DevOps crew needs to update their running containers in Google Kubernetes Engine (GKE) How must the DevOps crew do this?

A. Use Puppet or Chef to push out the patch to the running container.

B. Verify that auto upgrade is enabled; if so, Google will upgrade the nodes in a GKE cluster.

C. Update the application code or apply a patch, build a new image, and redeploy it.

D. Organize containers to automatically upgrade when the base image is available in Container Registry.

QUESTION 35

For compliance reasons, an organization needs to make sure that in-scope PCI Kubernetes Pods reside on "in-scope" Nodes only. These Nodes can only contain the "in-scope" Pods.

How must the organization achieve this objective?

A. Add a nodeSelector field to the pod configuration to only use the Nodes labeled inscope: accurate.

B. Make a node pool with the label inscope: accurate and a Pod Security Policy that only lets the Pods to run on Nodes with that label.

C. Place a taint on the Nodes with the label inscope: accurate and effect NoSchedule and a toleration to match in the Pod configuration.

D. Run all in-scope Pods in the namespace "in-scope-pci".

QUESTION 36

In an effort for your corporation messaging app to comply with FIPS 140-2, a decision was made to use GCP compute and network services. The messaging app architecture includes a Managed Instance Group (MIG) that controls a cluster of Compute Engine instances. The instances use Local SSDs for data caching and UDP for instance-to-instance communications. The app development crew is willing to make any changes necessary to comply with the standard

Which options must you suggest to meet the necessities?

A. Encrypt all cache storage and VM-to-VM communication using the BoringCrypto module.
B. Set Disk Encryption on the Instance Template used by the MIG to `client-managed key` and use BoringSSL for all data transit among instances.
C. Change the app instance-to-instance communications from UDP to TCP and enable BoringSSL on clients' TLS connections.
D. Set Disk Encryption on the Instance Template used by the MIG to `Google-managed Key` and use BoringSSL library on all instance-to-instance communications.

QUESTION 37

A client has an analytics workload running on Compute Engine that must have limited internet access. Your crew made an egress firewall rule to deny (priority 1000) all traffic to the internet.
The Compute Engine instances now need to reach out to the public repository to get security updates. What must your crew do?

A. Make an egress firewall rule to allow traffic to the CIDR range of the repository with a priority greater than 1000.
B. Make an egress firewall rule to allow traffic to the CIDR range of the repository with a priority less than 1000.
C. Make an egress firewall rule to allow traffic to the hostname of the repository with a priority greater than 1000.
D. Make an egress firewall rule to allow traffic to the hostname of the repository with a priority less than 1000.

QUESTION 38

You want data on Compute Engine disks to be encrypted at rest with keys managed by Cloud Key Management Service (KMS). Cloud Identity and Access Management (IAM) permissions to these keys needs to be managed in a grouped way for the reason that the permissions must be the same for all keys.

What must you do?

A. Make a single KeyRing for all persistent disks and all Keys in this KeyRing. Manage the IAM permissions at the Key level.
B. Make a single KeyRing for all persistent disks and all Keys in this KeyRing. Manage the IAM permissions at the KeyRing level.
C. Make a KeyRing per persistent disk, with each Keying containing a single Key. Manage the IAM permissions at the Key level.
D. Make a KeyRing per persistent disk, with each KeyRing containing a single Key. Manage the IAM permissions at the KeyRing level.

QUESTION 39

A client terminates an engineer and needs to make sure the engineer's Google account is automatically deprovisioned. What must the client do?

A. Use the Cloud SDK with their directory service to eliminate their IAM permissions in Cloud Identity.

B. Use the Cloud SDK with their directory service to provision and deprovision users from Cloud Identity.

C. Organize Cloud Directory Sync with their directory service to provision and deprovision users from Cloud Identity.

D. Organize Cloud Directory Sync with their directory service to eliminate their IAM permissions in Cloud Identity.

QUESTION 40

Which international compliance standard offers guidelines for information security controls applicable to the provision and use of cloud services?

A. ISO 27001
B. ISO 27002
C. ISO 27017
D. ISO 27018

QUESTION 41

An organization is starting to move its infrastructure from its on-premises environment to Google Cloud Platform (GCP). The first step the organization necessitates to take is to migrate its ongoing data backup and disaster recovery results to GCP. The organization's on-premises production environment is going to be the next phase for migration to GCP. Stable networking connectivity among the on-premises environment and GCP is also being implemented. Which GCP result must the organization use?

A. BigQuery using a data pipeline job with continuous updates via Cloud VPN

B. Cloud Storage using a scheduled task and gsutil via Cloud Interconnect

C. Compute Engines Virtual Machines using Persistent Disk via Cloud Interconnect

D. Cloud Datastore using regularly scheduled batch upload jobs via Cloud VPN

QUESTION 42

What are the steps to encrypt data using envelope encryption?

A. Make a data encryption key (DEK) locally. Use a key encryption key (KEK) to wrap the DEK. Encrypt data with the KEK.
B. Store the encrypted data and the wrapped KEK.
C. Make a key encryption key (KEK) locally.
D. Use the KEK to make a data encryption key (DEK). Encrypt data with the DEK.
E. Store the encrypted data and the wrapped DEK.
F. Make a data encryption key (DEK) locally. Encrypt data with the DEK.
G. Use a key encryption key (KEK) to wrap the DEK. Store the encrypted data and the wrapped DEK.
H. Make a key encryption key (KEK) locally. Make a data encryption key (DEK) locally. Encrypt data with the KEK

QUESTION 43

A client necessitates to make it convenient for their mobile workforce to access a CRM web interface that is hosted on Google Cloud Platform (GCP). The CRM can only be opened by someone on the corporate network. The client necessitates to make it available over the internet. Your crew necessitates an verification layer in front of the application that supports two-factor verification

Which GCP product must the client implement to meet these necessities?

A. Cloud Identity-Aware Proxy
B. Cloud Armor
C. Cloud Endpoints
D. Cloud VPN

QUESTION 44

Your corporation is storing sensitive data in Cloud Storage. You

want a key made on-premises to be used in the encryption

process. What must you do?

A. Use the Cloud Key Management Service to manage a data
   encryption key (DEK).
B. Use the Cloud Key Management Service to manage a key
   encryption key (KEK).
C. Use client-supplied encryption keys to manage the data
   encryption key (DEK).
D. Use client-supplied encryption keys to manage the key
   encryption key (KEK).

QUESTION 45

Your crew necessitates to limit users with administrative

opportunities at the organization level Which two roles must

your crew restrict? (Select two.)

A. Organization Administrator
B. Super Admin
C. GKE Cluster Admin
D. Compute Admin
E. Organization Role Viewer

ANSWERS

1. **Correct Answer: BC**
   Explanation/Reference:
   Reference: https://cloud.google.com/solutions/best-practices-for-building-containers
2. **Correct Answer: DE**
   Explanation/Reference:
   Reference: https://cloud.google.com/solutions/secure-data-workloads-use-cases
3. **Correct Answer: A**
4. **Correct Answer: C**
   Reference: https://cloud.google.com/blog/products/gcp/dnssec-now-available-in-cloud-dns
5. **Correct Answer: C**
   Reference: https://cloud.google.com/security-scanner/
6. **Correct Answer: C**
7. **Correct Answer: C**
8.
9. **Correct Answer: B**
10. **Correct Answer: A**
    Reference: https://cloud.google.com/kms/docs/envelope-encryption
11. **Correct Answer: C**
12. **Correct Answer: D**
    Reference; https://cloud.google.com/dlp/docs/deidentify-sensitive-data
13. **Correct Answer: C**
    Reference: https://cloud.google.com/iam/docs/understanding-service-accounts
14. **Correct Answer: B**
15. **Correct Answer: A**
16. **Correct Answer: D**
17. **Correct Answer: C**
    Reference:https://cloud.google.com/vpc/docs/shared-vpc

18. Correct Answer: A
19. Correct Answer: B
    Reference:https://cloud.google.com/kubernetes-engine/docs/how-to/dynamic-provisioning-cmek
20. Correct Answer: D
    Reference: https://cloud.google.com/storage/docs/encryption/customer-supplied-keys
21. Correct Answer: BD
22. Correct Answer: D
    Reference:https://cloud.google.com/solutions/best-practices-for-building-containers
23. Correct Answer: B
    Reference: https://cloud.google.com/blog/products/identity-security/using-your-existing-identity-management-system-with-google-cloud-platform
24. Correct Answer: D
25. Correct Answer: B
    Reference: https://cloud.google.com/bigquery/docs/locations
26. Correct Answer: A
27. Correct Answer: C
28. Correct Answer: D
    Reference: https://cloud.google.com/load-balancing/docs/ssl/
29. Correct Answer: BD
30. Correct Answer: D
31. Correct Answer: D
32. Correct Answer: B
33. Correct Answer: C
    Reference: https://cloud.google.com/compute/docs/ip-addresses/reserve-static-external-ip-address
34. Correct Answer: B
    Reference: https://cloud.google.com/kubernetes-engine/docs/security-bulletins
35. Correct Answer: C
36. Correct Answer: D
37. Correct Answer: C
38. Correct Answer: C
39. Correct Answer: C
40. Correct Answer: C

41. **Correct Answer: B**
    Reference:
    https://cloud.google.com/solutions/migration-to-google-cloud-building-your-foundation
42. **Correct Answer: C**
    Reference:
    https://cloud.google.com/kms/docs/envelope-encryption
43. **Correct Answer: D**
44. **Correct Answer: A**
    Reference:
    https://cloud.google.com/security/encryption-at-rest/default-encryption/
45. **Correct Answer: AB**
    Reference: https://cloud.google.com/resource-manager/docs/creating-managing-organization.